**EQUIPPING THE SAINTS
BIBLE SCHOOL**

EPHESIANS 4:11-16

Course: Spiritual Growth

Equipping the Saints Bible School

Course: Spiritual Growth

Copyright © 2019 Equipping the Saints Bible School

ISBN: 9781691082124

Table of Contents

Overview of the School

Equipping the Saints (ETS) Bible School is a two-year Bible School that is designed to help equip you for ministry. It's not only a school that teaches you the word of God, but also teaches you how to be a doer of it.

Certificate of Completion will be granted to each student who completes the "Theology & Great Commission" course.

Course: Foundations of Theology   **(Lengthen of course: 9 months)**

During this course, you will learn about many foundational Christian doctrines that we as believers build our faith upon. These doctrines include: The Fall of Man, The Holy inspiration of the Bible, The Plan of Salvation, The Trinity, Sanctification, Divine Healing, The End Times etc. In regards to an elder/bishop, Titus 1:9 says, "holding fast the faithful word as he has been taught, that he may be able, by sound doctrine, both to exhort and convict those who contradict." Paul wrote in 2 Timothy 2:24, "And a servant of the Lord must not quarrel but be gentle to all, able to teach, patient," And James writes, "My brethren, let not many of you become teachers, knowing that we shall receive a stricter judgment." (James 3:1). This course will equip you with a strong understanding of the Bible so that you are able to teach sound doctrine.

Course: The Great Commission   **(Length of course: 6 months)**

The Great Commission is summed up in preaching the gospel (Mark 16:15) and making disciples (Matthew 28:19). Jesus gave these commandments to all believers. In this course you will learn how to effectively preach the gospel, be a soul winner, and make disciples. Our teachers have been very fruitful in these areas so you will gain great insight from their teachings and experiences. This course will help equip you to be an effective soul winner and disciple maker.

Advanced Certificate of Completion will be granted to each student who completes the "Spiritual Growth & Family Life" courses in addition to the "Theology & Great Commission" course.

Course: Spiritual Growth   **(Length of course: 3 months)**

This course is designed to help you grow in your walk with God by allowing the Lord to deeply examine your heart. You will learn about one of the most deceptive snares Satan uses to get believers out of the will of God, i.e. offense. This trap restrains countless Christians, severs relationships, and causes many to bounce from one church to another. Everyone will encounter offense, so it is not a matter of if, rather, when you will encounter it. But, through this course, when you do encounter offense, you will know how to react so that you can overcome it and grow from the opportunity. Also, you will learn how to find healing from past hurts that you may still be struggling with. This is so important because hurt people, hurt people. God wants you to minister from a place of healing. And the only way that can take place is if you are first healed.

You will also learn why we as believers must be submitted to God's sovereign authority, as well as the blessings that result from doing so. You will study how submission to this divine order grants the Kingdom's provision and protection for your life.

By the completion of this course your character will be transformed, making you into a powerful disciple!

Course: Family Life   **(Length of course: 6 months)**

In 1 Timothy 3:1-7, the Apostle Paul highlights many qualities needed in the life of a bishop. These qualities include, being a husband to one wife and a man who rules his house well, with submissive children that show reverence to him. For these reasons, we have dedicated a whole course to the Christian family life. We believe Christian leaders should have model households. You will also learn about how to have a strong marriage while being active in ministry.

Another area this course covers is Biblical finances. We believe the word of God gives the greatest instruction on how to manage our money. You will be given a structured plan how to become debt free and learn how to budget well so you can experience financial freedom. Having your finances in order is very important, not only to remove stress from your life, but also to enable you to do all that God has called you to do for His Kingdom.

In each course, you will be encouraged to maintain a strong, daily walk with God comprised of reading your Bible and praying. We believe everything you ever will accomplish starts with your daily walk with God. Students will be challenged to make evangelism a part of their everyday life. We believe evangelism is a lifestyle, not something you only do when the church has a scheduled outreach. By completing this school, you will be a well-equipped saint to help build the body of Christ and win the world for Jesus!

Please note: Equipping the Saints Bible School is not an accredited institution nor are any of the classes therein transferable.

Weekly Assignments

- Read the daily assigned chapter(s) from the Bible.

- Every morning set aside time to get alone with God to pray for at least 30 minutes.

- Read the chapter(s) from the assigned book and write a summary of what you read from each chapter.

- Memorize the assigned Scripture(s). It is important that you do not wait until the last minute to memorize the verse of the week. This approach will only produce short-term memory. The best way to log the verse into your long-term memory is to start early in the week and meditate on the verse throughout the day. A good way to do this is to write the verse on a flashcard and look at it throughout the day.

- Carry tracts/flyers everywhere you go and personally invite five different people to church every week.

- Attend the weekly class and take notes.

- Complete weekly assignment.

- Have an accountability partner check the boxes, signifying you've completed your homework.

Extra Note: For this course, you will need a NKJV Bible. All questions that you fill in the blanks are in the NKJV unless otherwise notated.

Name of the Student

_____

The Importance of Having a Daily Walk of Reading Your Bible and Praying

Things You Should do When You're Reading the Word of God

- Ask the Holy Spirit to open the eyes of your understanding and give you ears to hear what He's saying to you through the Scriptures.

- As you read, underline/highlight verses in the Bible that stand out and speak to you. You should keep a small notebook beside you when you read and write down the thoughts the Lord gives to you or questions you may have about certain Scriptures you come across. Later, you can speak with a church leader about them.

- Read the Word until you gain meaning and understanding. Don't let your mind wander to other things; concentrate on what you are reading. Don't just read the words at the surface. Look for the deeper meaning in the passage. Ask yourself continually, "How does this apply to my life right now? What is God saying to me? What is the true meaning of these verses?"

- We recommend you buy one of the following Bible commentaries: New Spirit-Filled Life Bible, Life Application Study Bible, Nelson Study Bible, or Life in the Spirit Study Bible.

Steps to Developing a Strong Prayer Life

- Start your morning by setting aside time where you get alone with God and pray (a time where you give Him your undivided attention and have intimacy) (Matthew 6:6). As you do this every day, your prayer time will begin to expand, and soon, you will be praying for hours! (This doesn't mean this is the only time you're to pray. You need to pray throughout the day—pray without ceasing!)

- We always tell people who want to pray but don't know what to pray for, to make a prayer list before they start praying—a list of things that they know needs their prayers. (Unsaved loved ones, your family, old friends, and strength to walk in victory over temptation; thank the Lord for all that He has done, pray for missionaries, your pastor(s) and leaders at the church, pray for those that you know are hurting and struggling. This is just a small list of things to start with—make your own list. Also, you can use the Lord's Prayer as an outline. See Matthew 6:9-13).

- Remember that prayer is simply talking to God. You communicate with God in much the same way you interact with another person, but with reverence knowing that He is God.

- Sin in our lives will hinder our prayers. Make sure you examine your heart and confess your sins. You don't want your prayers to be hindered.

Daily Bible reading: Read the chapter and then check the box after you've read it.

[] Matthew chapter 1

[] Matthew chapter 2

[] Matthew chapter 3

[] Matthew chapter 4

[] Matthew chapter 5

[] Matthew chapter 6

[] Matthew chapter 7

Daily Prayer Time: Every morning, set aside at least 30 minutes to have alone time with God in prayer. Check the box after you've finished praying each morning.

[] I prayed for at least 30 minutes this morning.

[] I prayed for at least 30 minutes this morning.

[] I prayed for at least 30 minutes this morning.

[] I prayed for at least 30 minutes this morning.

[] I prayed for at least 30 minutes this morning.

[] I prayed for at least 30 minutes this morning.

[] I prayed for at least 30 minutes this morning.

Memory verse for week 1

Romans 13:1: Let every soul be subject to the governing authorities. For there is no authority except from God, and the authorities that exist are appointed by God.

[] I carried tracts/flyers with me and personally invited five different people to church this week.

[] Accountability partner checks the box if weekly homework was completed.

Classroom Notes

Week 1

Title: _____

Scriptures quoted: _____

_____

_____

Notes/What spoke to you? _____

_____

_____

_____

_____

_____

_____

_____

_____

_____

_____

_____

_____

_____

[] Accountability partner checks the box if the work was completed.

Week 1: Under Cover: Why Your Response to Leadership Determines Your Future

Read Chapters 1-3

Chapter 1 Summary: _____

_____

_____

_____

_____

_____

_____

_____

_____

_____

_____

_____

What spoke to you personally? _____

_____

_____

_____

_____

_____

_____

_____

Chapter 2 Summary: _____

_____

_____

_____

_____

_____

_____

_____

_____

What spoke to you personally? _____

_____

_____

_____

_____

_____

_____

Chapter 3 Summary: _____

_____

_____

_____

_____

_____

_____

_____

_____

_____

What spoke to you personally? _____

_____

_____

_____

_____

_____

_____

[] Accountability partner checks the box if the work was completed.

Daily Bible reading: Read the chapter and then check the box after you've read it.

[] Matthew chapter 8

[] Matthew chapter 9

[] Matthew chapter 10

[] Matthew chapter 11

[] Matthew chapter 12

[] Matthew chapter 13

[] Matthew chapter 14

Daily Prayer Time: Every morning, set aside at least 30 minutes to have alone time with God in prayer. Check the box after you've finished praying each morning.

[] I prayed for at least 30 minutes this morning.

[] I prayed for at least 30 minutes this morning.

[] I prayed for at least 30 minutes this morning.

[] I prayed for at least 30 minutes this morning.

[] I prayed for at least 30 minutes this morning.

[] I prayed for at least 30 minutes this morning.

[] I prayed for at least 30 minutes this morning.

Memory verse for week 2

Hebrews 13:7: Remember those who rule over you, who have spoken the word of God to you, whose faith follow, considering the outcome of their conduct.

[] I carried tracts/flyers with me and personally invited five different people to church this week.

[] Accountability partner checks the box if the work was completed.

Classroom Notes

Week 2

Title: _____

Scriptures quoted: _____

_____

_____

Notes/What spoke to you? _____

_____

_____

_____

_____

_____

_____

_____

_____

_____

_____

_____

_____

[] Accountability partner checks the box if the work was completed.

Week 2: Under Cover: Why Your Response to Leadership Determines Your Future

Read Chapters 4-6

Chapter 4 Summary: _____

_____

_____

_____

_____

_____

_____

_____

_____

_____

_____

What spoke to you personally? _____

_____

_____

_____

_____

_____

_____

_____

Chapter 5 Summary: _____

_____

_____

_____

_____

_____

_____

_____

_____

_____

What spoke to you personally? _____

_____

_____

_____

_____

_____

_____

_____

Chapter 6 Summary: _____

_____

_____

_____

_____

_____

_____

_____

_____

What spoke to you personally? _____

_____

_____

_____

_____

_____

_____

_____

_____

[] Accountability partner checks the box if the work was completed.

Daily Bible reading: Read the chapter and then check the box after you've read it.

[] Matthew chapter 15

[] Matthew chapter 16

[] Matthew chapter 17

[] Matthew chapter 18

[] Matthew chapter 19

[] Matthew chapter 20

[] Matthew chapter 21

Daily Prayer Time: Every morning, set aside at least 30 minutes to have alone time with God in prayer. Check the box after you've finished praying each morning.

[] I prayed for at least 30 minutes this morning.

[] I prayed for at least 30 minutes this morning.

[] I prayed for at least 30 minutes this morning.

[] I prayed for at least 30 minutes this morning.

[] I prayed for at least 30 minutes this morning.

[] I prayed for at least 30 minutes this morning.

[] I prayed for at least 30 minutes this morning.

Memory verse for week 3

Hebrews 13:17: Obey those who rule over you, and be submissive, for they watch out for your souls, as those who must give account. Let them do so with joy and not with grief, for that would be unprofitable for you.

[] I carried tracts/flyers with me and personally invited five different people to church this week.

[] Accountability partner checks the box if the work was completed.

Classroom Notes

Week 3

Title: _____

Scriptures quoted: _____

_____

_____

Notes/What spoke to you? _____

_____

_____

_____

_____

_____

_____

_____

_____

_____

_____

_____

_____

[] Accountability partner checks the box if the work was completed.

Week 3: Under Cover: Why Your Response to Leadership Determines Your Future

Read Chapters 7-9

Chapter 7 Summary: _____

_____

_____

_____

_____

_____

_____

_____

_____

_____

What spoke to you personally? _____

_____

_____

_____

_____

_____

_____

Chapter 8 Summary: _____

_____

_____

_____

_____

_____

_____

_____

_____

_____

_____

What spoke to you personally? _____

_____

_____

_____

_____

_____

_____

_____

_____

_____

_____

Chapter 9 Summary: _____

_____

_____

_____

_____

_____

_____

_____

_____

_____

What spoke to you personally? _____

_____

_____

_____

_____

_____

_____

[] Accountability partner checks the box if the work was completed.

Daily Bible reading: Read the chapter and then check the box after you've read it.

[] Matthew chapter 22

[] Matthew chapter 23

[] Matthew chapter 24

[] Matthew chapter 25

[] Matthew chapter 26

[] Matthew chapter 27

[] Matthew chapter 28

Daily Prayer Time: Every morning, set aside at least 30 minutes to have alone time with God in prayer. Check the box after you've finished praying each morning.

[] I prayed for at least 30 minutes this morning.

[] I prayed for at least 30 minutes this morning.

[] I prayed for at least 30 minutes this morning.

[] I prayed for at least 30 minutes this morning.

[] I prayed for at least 30 minutes this morning.

[] I prayed for at least 30 minutes this morning.

[] I prayed for at least 30 minutes this morning.

Memory verse for week 4

1 Timothy 5:19: Do not receive an accusation against an elder except from two or three witnesses.

[] I carried tracts/flyers with me and personally invited five different people to church this week.

[] Accountability partner checks the box if the work was completed.

Classroom Notes

Week 4

Title: _____

Scriptures quoted: _____

_____

_____

Notes/What spoke to you? _____

_____

_____

_____

_____

_____

_____

_____

_____

_____

_____

_____

_____

_____

_____

[] Accountability partner checks the box if the work was completed.

Week 4: Under Cover: Why Your Response to Leadership Determines Your Future

Read Chapters 10-12

Chapter 10 Summary: _____

_____

_____

_____

_____

_____

_____

_____

_____

_____

What spoke to you personally? _____

_____

_____

_____

_____

_____

_____

_____

_____

Chapter 11 Summary: _____

_____

_____

_____

_____

_____

_____

_____

_____

_____

What spoke to you personally? _____

_____

_____

_____

_____

_____

_____

_____

Chapter 12 Summary: _____

_____

_____

_____

_____

_____

_____

_____

_____

_____

What spoke to you personally? _____

_____

_____

_____

_____

_____

_____

[] Accountability partner checks the box if the work was completed.

Daily Bible reading: Read the chapter and then check the box after you've read it.

[] 1 Corinthians chapter 1

[] 1 Corinthians chapter 2

[] 1 Corinthians chapter 3

[] 1 Corinthians chapter 4

[] 1 Corinthians chapter 5

[] 1 Corinthians chapter 6

[] 1 Corinthians chapter 7

Daily Prayer Time: Every morning, set aside at least 30 minutes to have alone time with God in prayer. Check the box after you've finished praying each morning.

[] I prayed for at least 30 minutes this morning.

[] I prayed for at least 30 minutes this morning.

[] I prayed for at least 30 minutes this morning.

[] I prayed for at least 30 minutes this morning.

[] I prayed for at least 30 minutes this morning.

[] I prayed for at least 30 minutes this morning.

[] I prayed for at least 30 minutes this morning.

Memory verse for week 5

1 Thessalonians 5:12-13: And we urge you, brethren, to recognize those who labor among you, and are over you in the Lord and admonish you, [13] and to esteem them very highly in love for their work's sake. Be at peace among yourselves.

[] I carried tracts/flyers with me and personally invited five different people to church this week.

[] Accountability partner checks the box if the work was completed.

Classroom Notes

Week 5

Title: _____

Scriptures quoted: _____

_____

_____

Notes/What spoke to you? _____

_____

_____

_____

_____

_____

_____

_____

_____

_____

_____

_____

_____

_____

[] Accountability partner check the box if the work was completed.

Week 5: Under Cover: Why Your Response to Leadership Determines Your Future

Read Chapters 13-14

Chapter 13 Summary: _____

_____

_____

_____

_____

_____

_____

_____

_____

_____

_____

What spoke to you personally? _____

_____

_____

_____

_____

_____

_____

_____

Chapter 14 Summary: _____

_____

_____

_____

_____

_____

_____

_____

_____

_____

_____

What spoke to you personally? _____

_____

_____

_____

_____

_____

_____

[] Accountability partner checks the box if the work was completed.

Daily Bible reading: Read the chapter and then check the box after you've read it.

[] 1 Corinthians chapter 8

[] 1 Corinthians chapter 9

[] 1 Corinthians chapter 10

[] 1 Corinthians chapter 11

[] 1 Corinthians chapter 12

[] 1 Corinthians chapter 13

[] 1 Corinthians chapter 14

Daily Prayer Time: Every morning, set aside at least 30 minutes to have alone time with God in prayer. Check the box after you've finished praying each morning.

[] I prayed for at least 30 minutes this morning.

[] I prayed for at least 30 minutes this morning.

[] I prayed for at least 30 minutes this morning.

[] I prayed for at least 30 minutes this morning.

[] I prayed for at least 30 minutes this morning.

[] I prayed for at least 30 minutes this morning.

[] I prayed for at least 30 minutes this morning.

Memory verse for week 6

1 Peter 2:17: Honor all people. Love the brotherhood. Fear God. Honor the king.

[] I carried tracts/flyers with me and personally invited five different people to church this week.

[] Accountability partner checks the box if the work was completed.

Classroom Notes

Week 6

Title: _____

Scriptures quoted: _____

_____

_____

Notes/What spoke to you? _____

_____

_____

_____

_____

_____

_____

_____

_____

_____

_____

_____

_____

[] Accountability partner checks the box if the work was completed.

Week 6: Under Cover: Why Your Response to Leadership Determines Your Future

Read Chapters 15-18

Chapter 15 Summary: _____

_____

_____

_____

_____

_____

_____

_____

_____

_____

_____

What spoke to you personally? _____

_____

_____

_____

_____

_____

_____

_____

Chapter 16 Summary: _____

_____

_____

_____

_____

_____

_____

_____

_____

_____

_____

What spoke to you personally? _____

_____

_____

_____

_____

_____

_____

_____

_____

Chapter 17 Summary: _____

_____

_____

_____

_____

_____

_____

_____

_____

_____

What spoke to you personally? _____

_____

_____

_____

_____

_____

_____

_____

Chapter 18 Summary: _____

_____

_____

_____

_____

_____

_____

_____

_____

_____

What spoke to you personally? _____

_____

_____

_____

_____

_____

_____

_____

[] Accountability partner checks the box if the work was completed.

Daily Bible reading: Read the chapter and then check the box after you've read it.

[] 1 Corinthians chapter 15

[] 1 Corinthians chapter 16

[] 2 Corinthians chapter 1

[] 2 Corinthians chapter 2

[] 2 Corinthians chapter 3

[] 2 Corinthians chapter 4

[] 2 Corinthians chapter 5

Daily Prayer Time: Every morning, set aside at least 30 minutes to have alone time with God in prayer. Check the box after you've finished praying each morning.

[] I prayed for at least 30 minutes this morning.

[] I prayed for at least 30 minutes this morning.

[] I prayed for at least 30 minutes this morning.

[] I prayed for at least 30 minutes this morning.

[] I prayed for at least 30 minutes this morning.

[] I prayed for at least 30 minutes this morning.

[] I prayed for at least 30 minutes this morning.

Memory verse for week 7

Ephesians 4:32: And be kind to one another, tenderhearted, forgiving one another, even as God in Christ forgave you.

[] I carried tracts/flyers with me and personally invited five different people to church this week.

[] Accountability partner checks the box if the work was completed.

Classroom Notes

Week 7

Title: _____

Scriptures quoted: _____

_____

_____

Notes/What spoke to you? _____

_____

_____

_____

_____

_____

_____

_____

_____

_____

_____

_____

_____

[] Accountability partner checks the box if the work was completed.

Week 7: The Bait of Satan: Living Free from the Deadly Trap of Offense

Read Chapters 1-2

Chapter 1 Summary: _____

_____

_____

_____

_____

_____

_____

_____

_____

_____

_____

What spoke to you personally? _____

_____

_____

_____

_____

_____

_____

_____

Chapter 2 Summary: _____

_____

_____

_____

_____

_____

_____

_____

_____

_____

What spoke to you personally? _____

_____

_____

_____

_____

_____

_____

[] Accountability partner checks the box if the work was completed.

Daily Bible reading: Read the chapter and then check the box after you've read it.

[] 2 Corinthians chapter 6

[] 2 Corinthians chapter 7

[] 2 Corinthians chapter 8

[] 2 Corinthians chapter 9

[] 2 Corinthians chapter 10

[] 2 Corinthians chapter 11

[] 2 Corinthians chapter 12

Daily Prayer Time: Every morning, set aside at least 30 minutes to have alone time with God in prayer. Check the box after you've finished praying each morning.

[] I prayed for at least 30 minutes this morning.

[] I prayed for at least 30 minutes this morning.

[] I prayed for at least 30 minutes this morning.

[] I prayed for at least 30 minutes this morning.

[] I prayed for at least 30 minutes this morning.

[] I prayed for at least 30 minutes this morning.

[] I prayed for at least 30 minutes this morning.

Memory verse for week 8

Matthew 6:14: "For if you forgive men their trespasses, your heavenly Father will also forgive you.

[] I carried tracts/flyers with me and personally invited five different people to church this week.

[] Accountability partner checks the box if the work was completed.

Classroom Notes

Week 8

Title: _____

Scriptures quoted: _____

_____

_____

Notes/What spoke to you? _____

_____

_____

_____

_____

_____

_____

_____

_____

_____

_____

_____

_____

[] Accountability partner checks the box if the work was completed.

Week 8: The Bait of Satan: Living Free from the Deadly Trap of Offense

Read Chapters 3-4

Chapter 3 Summary: _____

_____

_____

_____

_____

_____

_____

_____

_____

_____

_____

_____

What spoke to you personally? _____

_____

_____

_____

_____

_____

_____

_____

_____

Chapter 4 Summary: _____

_____

_____

_____

_____

_____

_____

_____

_____

What spoke to you personally? _____

_____

_____

_____

_____

_____

_____

[] Accountability partner checks the box if the work was completed.

Daily Bible reading: Read the chapter and then check the box after you've read it.

[] 2 Corinthians chapter 13

[] Galatians chapter 1

[] Galatians chapter 2

[] Galatians chapter 3

[] Galatians chapter 4

[] Galatians chapter 5

[] Galatians chapter 6

Daily Prayer Time: Every morning, set aside at least 30 minutes to have alone time with God in prayer. Check the box after you've finished praying each morning.

[] I prayed for at least 30 minutes this morning.

[] I prayed for at least 30 minutes this morning.

[] I prayed for at least 30 minutes this morning.

[] I prayed for at least 30 minutes this morning.

[] I prayed for at least 30 minutes this morning.

[] I prayed for at least 30 minutes this morning.

[] I prayed for at least 30 minutes this morning.

Memory verse for week 9

Colossians 3:13: bearing with one another, and forgiving one another, if anyone has a complaint against another; even as Christ forgave you, so you also must do.

[] I carried tracts/flyers with me and personally invited five different people to church this week.

[] Accountability partner checks the box if the work was completed.

Classroom Notes

Week 9

Title: _____

Scriptures quoted: _____

_____

_____

Notes/What spoke to you? _____

_____

_____

_____

_____

_____

_____

_____

_____

_____

_____

_____

_____

[] Accountability partner checks the box if the work was completed.

Week 9: The Bait of Satan: Living Free from the Deadly Trap of Offense

Read Chapters 5-6

Chapter 5 Summary: _____

_____

_____

_____

_____

_____

_____

_____

_____

_____

What spoke to you personally? _____

_____

_____

_____

_____

_____

_____

Chapter 6 Summary: _____

_____

_____

_____

_____

_____

_____

_____

_____

What spoke to you personally? _____

_____

_____

_____

_____

_____

_____

[] Accountability partner checks the box if the work was completed.

Daily Bible reading: Read the chapter(s) and then check the box after you've read it.

[] Philippians chapter 1

[] Philippians chapter 2

[] Philippians chapter 3

[] Philippians chapter 4

[] Colossians chapter 1

[] Colossians chapter 2

[] Colossians chapter 3-4

Daily Prayer Time: Every morning, set aside at least 30 minutes to have alone time with God in prayer. Check the box after you've finished praying each morning.

[] I prayed for at least 30 minutes this morning.

[] I prayed for at least 30 minutes this morning.

[] I prayed for at least 30 minutes this morning.

[] I prayed for at least 30 minutes this morning.

[] I prayed for at least 30 minutes this morning.

[] I prayed for at least 30 minutes this morning.

[] I prayed for at least 30 minutes this morning.

Memory verse for week 10

Matthew 18:21-22: Then Peter came to Him and said, "Lord, how often shall my brother sin against me, and I forgive him? Up to seven times?" [22] Jesus said to him, "I do not say to you, up to seven times, but up to seventy times seven.

[] I carried tracts/flyers with me and personally invited five different people to church this week.

[] Accountability partner checks the box if the work was completed.

Classroom Notes

Week 10

Title: _____

Scriptures quoted: _____

_____

_____

Notes/What spoke to you? _____

_____

_____

_____

_____

_____

_____

_____

_____

_____

_____

_____

_____

[] Accountability partner checks the box if the work was completed.

Week 10: The Bait of Satan: Living Free from the Deadly Trap of Offense

Read Chapters 7-8

Chapter 7 Summary: _____

_____

_____

_____

_____

_____

_____

_____

_____

_____

What spoke to you personally? _____

_____

_____

_____

_____

_____

_____

_____

Chapter 8 Summary: _____

_____

_____

_____

_____

_____

_____

_____

_____

_____

What spoke to you personally? _____

_____

_____

_____

_____

_____

_____

[] Accountability partner checks the box if the work was completed.

Daily Bible reading: Read the chapter and then check the box after you've read it.

[] 1 Thessalonians chapter 1

[] 1 Thessalonians chapter 2

[] 1 Thessalonians chapter 3

[] 1 Thessalonians chapter 4

[] 1 Thessalonians chapter 5

[] 2 Thessalonians chapter 1

[] 2 Thessalonians chapter 2

Daily Prayer Time: Every morning, set aside at least 30 minutes to have alone time with God in prayer. Check the box after you've finished praying each morning.

[] I prayed for at least 30 minutes this morning.

[] I prayed for at least 30 minutes this morning.

[] I prayed for at least 30 minutes this morning.

[] I prayed for at least 30 minutes this morning.

[] I prayed for at least 30 minutes this morning.

[] I prayed for at least 30 minutes this morning.

[] I prayed for at least 30 minutes this morning.

Memory verse for week 11

Mark 11:25: "And whenever you stand praying, if you have anything against anyone, forgive him, that your Father in heaven may also forgive you your trespasses.

[] I carried tracts/flyers with me and personally invited five different people to church this week.

[] Accountability partner checks the box if the work was completed.

Classroom Notes

Week 11

Title: _____

Scriptures quoted: _____

_____

_____

Notes/What spoke to you? _____

_____

_____

_____

_____

_____

_____

_____

_____

_____

_____

_____

_____

_____

_____

[] Accountability partner checks the box if the work was completed.

Week 11: The Bait of Satan: Living Free from the Deadly Trap of Offense

Read Chapters 9-11

Chapter 9 Summary: _____

_____

_____

_____

_____

_____

_____

_____

_____

_____

What spoke to you personally? _____

_____

_____

_____

_____

_____

_____

_____

Chapter 10 Summary: _____

_____

_____

_____

_____

_____

_____

_____

_____

_____

What spoke to you personally? _____

_____

_____

_____

_____

_____

_____

_____

Chapter 11 Summary: _____

_____

_____

_____

_____

_____

_____

_____

_____

What spoke to you personally? _____

_____

_____

_____

_____

_____

[] Accountability partner checks the box if the work was completed.

Daily Bible reading: Read the chapter and then check the box after you've read it.

[] 2 Thessalonians chapter 3

[] Philemon chapter 1

[] James chapter 1

[] James chapter 2

[] James chapter 3

[] James chapter 4

[] James chapter 5

Daily Prayer Time: Every morning, set aside at least 30 minutes to have alone time with God in prayer. Check the box after you've finished praying each morning.

[] I prayed for at least 30 minutes this morning.

[] I prayed for at least 30 minutes this morning.

[] I prayed for at least 30 minutes this morning.

[] I prayed for at least 30 minutes this morning.

[] I prayed for at least 30 minutes this morning.

[] I prayed for at least 30 minutes this morning.

[] I prayed for at least 30 minutes this morning.

Memory verse for week 12

Matthew 6:12: And forgive us our debts, As we forgive our debtors.

[] I carried tracts/flyers with me and personally invited five different people to church this week.

[] Accountability partner checks the box if the work was completed.

Classroom Notes

Week 12

Title: _____

Scriptures quoted: _____

_____

_____

Notes/What spoke to you? _____

_____

_____

_____

_____

_____

_____

_____

_____

_____

_____

_____

_____

_____

[] Accountability partner checks the box if the work was completed.

Week 12: The Bait of Satan: Living Free from the Deadly Trap of Offense

Read Chapters 12-14

Chapter 12 Summary: _____

_____

_____

_____

_____

_____

_____

_____

_____

_____

_____

What spoke to you personally? _____

_____

_____

_____

_____

_____

_____

_____

Chapter 13 Summary: _____

_____

_____

_____

_____

_____

_____

_____

_____

_____

What spoke to you personally? _____

_____

_____

_____

_____

_____

_____

_____

_____

Chapter 14 Summary: _____

_____

_____

_____

_____

_____

_____

_____

_____

_____

What spoke to you personally? _____

_____

_____

_____

_____

_____

_____

[] Accountability partner checks the box if the work was completed.

The Absalom spirit of rebellion and disloyalty

Read 2 Sam 15:1-12

[1] There are basically 12 stages that an individual goes through when they have become influenced by the Absalom spirit of rebellion and disloyalty.

Ultimately, if not dealt with, the disloyalty that spreads through the congregation will bring a church split or the departure of many affected saints.

Here are the twelve stages:

1. **AN INDEPENDENT SPIRIT** – An attitude of independence emerges when the person no longer wants to serve the leadership but seeks recognition and a reputation.

2. **SELF-PROMOTION** – The person will maneuver for the praise of men. In II Samuel 15, Absalom stole the hearts of the people.

3. **SPIRITUAL PRIDE** – As people recognize and praise the deceived individual, he begins to believe that he is more spiritual than the leaders.

4. **AN OFFENDED SPIRIT** – The Absalom falls into an offended spirit because of spiritual pride. When his ideas and gifts are not promoted by the leadership as he believes they should be, he becomes highly offended. Often he will seek others that will agree with him in his offense.

5. **A CRITICAL SPIRIT** – Almost all the decisions of the leaders are questioned and undermined by the person. Sadly, with this critical spirit, the Absalom no longer can receive any spiritual feeding or direction from the leadership.

6. **A COMPETITIVE SPIRIT** – The Absalom sees himself in competition with the church leadership and begins to distort and misrepresent the decisions and directives the leaders are giving.

7. **SOWING STRIFE AND DIVISION** – The Absalom will take his offenses to many individuals in the church and spread his discontent through various means.

8. **ACCUSING THE LEADERSHIP** – The Absalom feeds his followers his critical spirit and faultfinding. Minor things, usually not related to God's spiritual qualifications, will be made major issues, such as what kind of car the pastor drives, how long he takes to receive the offerings, etc.

9. **OPEN DISLOYALTY AND DIVISION** – The Absalom feels that many are following him so he boldly brings his disloyalty out into the open. At this point, the leaders become aware of his

discontented splinter group. Now the people are forced to make a choice between the leaders of the church and the Absalom who has deceived them.

10. **A BOLD CONSPIRACY** – The Absalom justifies his conspiracy to everyone by focusing their attention on all the minor issues that he has found fault with in the leadership. (Usually, the Absalom does not have legitimate accusations such as the preaching of false doctrines or blatant sin on the part of the pastors.)

11. **A CHURCH SPLIT** – The Absalom leads a naive splinter group out to the birth of a new church or ministry. Declare a new vision.

12. **GOD'S JUDGMENT ON THE REBELLIOUS CHURCH** – The scripture tells us, "if the root be evil, the whole tree will be evil," and every church or ministry that is birthed by an Absalom spirit will be full of rebellion, disloyalty, and continual church splits.

What spoke to you personally? _____

_____

_____

_____

_____

_____

_____

_____

_____

_____

_____

_____

[] Accountability partner checks the box if the work was completed.

How did this course impact your walk with God? Write at least three paragraphs.

_____

_____

_____

_____

_____

_____

_____

_____

_____

_____

_____

_____

_____

_____

_____

_____

_____

_____

_____

_____

_____

_____

_____

_____

_____

_____

_____

_____

_____

_____

_____

_____

_____

_____

_____

_____

_____

_____

_____

_____

_____

[] Accountability partner checks the box if the work was completed

Footnote: 1. http://www.victorylifechurch.org/pdf/the_absalom_spirit.pdf

Made in the USA
Middletown, DE
29 March 2024

51927255R00040